it's Ukulele time

Learn how to play the ukulele using all-time favorite songs

Alfred Music
P.O. Box 10003
Van Nuys, CA 91410-0003
alfred.com

ISBN-10: 1-4706-1010-8
ISBN-13: 978-1-4706-1010-4

Cover Photo
Ukulele courtesy of Jennifer Harnsberger

 Alfred Cares. Contents printed on 100% recycled paper.

2

CONTENTS

SELECTING YOUR UKULELE

Ukuleles come in different types and sizes. There are four basic sizes: *soprano*, *concert*, *tenor*, and *baritone*. The smallest is the soprano, and they get gradually larger, with the baritone being the largest.

Soprano   Concert   Tenor   Baritone

Soprano, concert, and tenor ukuleles are all tuned to the same notes, but the baritone is tuned differently. Each ukulele has a different sound. The soprano has a light, soft sound, which is what you expect when you hear a ukulele. The larger the instrument, the deeper the sound is. Some tenor ukuleles have six or even eight strings.

The soprano ukulele is the most common, but you can use soprano, concert, and four-string tenor ukuleles with this book. Because the baritone ukulele is tuned to the same notes as the top four strings of the guitar, you can use *Learn to Play Baritone Uke* (Alfred #380) to start learning.

THE PARTS OF YOUR UKULELE

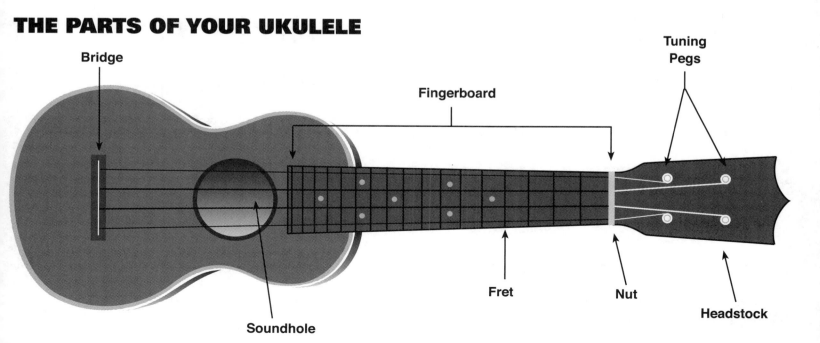

HOW TO TUNE YOUR UKULELE

Make sure your strings are wound properly around the tuning pegs. They should go from the inside to the outside, as in the picture.

Turning a tuning peg clockwise makes the pitch lower. Turning a tuning peg counter-clockwise makes the pitch higher. Be sure not to tune the strings too high because they could break!

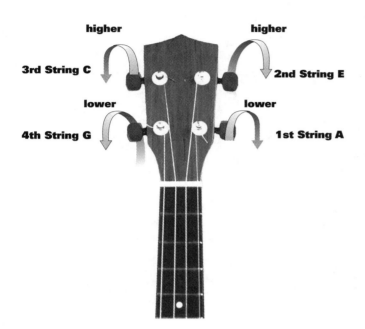

Important:

Always remember that the string closest to the floor is the 1st string. The one closest to the ceiling is the 4th string.

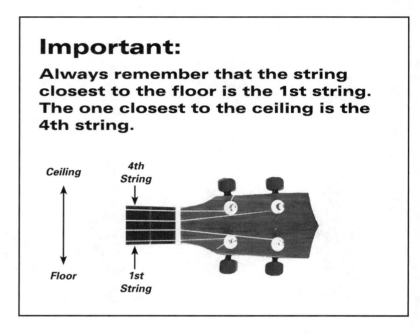

Tuning the Ukulele to Itself

When your 1st string is in tune, you can tune the rest of the strings just using the ukulele alone.
If you have a piano, or keyboard, available, tune the 1st string to A on the piano, then follow the instructions below to get the ukulele in tune.

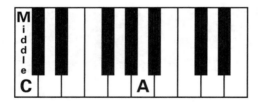

Press fret 5 of string 2 and tune it to the pitch of string 1 (A).

Press fret 4 of string 3 and tune it to the pitch of string 2 (E).

Press fret 2 of string 4 and tune it to the pitch of string 1 (A).

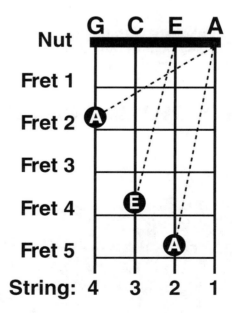

Pitch Pipes and Electronic Tuners

If you don't have a piano available, buying an electronic tuner or pitch pipe is recommended.
The salesperson at your local music store can show you how to use them. Tuning apps are also available for mobile devices.

HOW TO HOLD YOUR UKULELE

Standing

Cradle the ukulele with your right arm by gently holding it close to your body. Your right hand should be free to strum it. Keep your left wrist away from the fingerboard. This allows your fingers to be in a better position to finger the chords.

Sitting

Rest the ukulele gently on your thigh and gently hold it close to your body. Just like when you are standing, your right hand should be free for strumming; and remember to keep your left wrist away from the fingerboard.

THE RIGHT HAND: STRUMMING THE STRINGS

To *strum* means to play the strings with your right hand by brushing quickly across them. There are two common ways of strumming the strings. One is with a pick, and the other is with your fingers.

Strumming with a Pick

Hold the pick between your thumb and index finger. Hold it firmly, but don't squeeze it too hard.

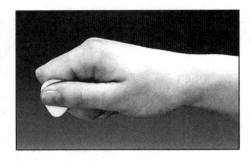

Strum from the 4th string (closest to the ceiling) to the 1st string (closest to the floor).

Important: Always strum by mostly moving your wrist, not just your arm. Use as little motion as possible. Start as close to the top strings as you can, and never let your hand move past the edge of the ukulele.

Start near the 4th string.

Move mostly your wrist, not just your arm.
Finish near the 1st string.

Strumming with Your Fingers

If you don't have a pick, you can strum with your fingers. Decide if you feel more comfortable strumming with the side of your thumb or the nail of your index finger. The strumming motion is the same with the thumb or finger as it is when using the pick. Strum from the 4th string to the 1st string.

Strumming with the thumb.

Strumming with the index finger.

Time to Strum!

Strum all four strings slowly and evenly. Count your strums out loud as you play. Repeat this exercise until you feel comfortable strumming the strings.

strum	strum	strum	strum	strum	strum	strum	strum
/	/	/	/	/	/	/	/

Count: 1 2 3 4 5 6 7 8

STRUMMING NOTATION

Beats

Each strum you play is equal to one *beat*. Beats are even, like the ticking of a clock.

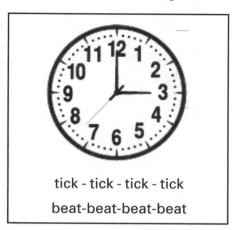

tick - tick - tick - tick

beat-beat-beat-beat

Introducing Slash Notation

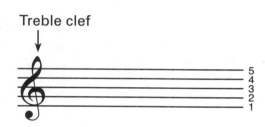

note name → C   /   /   / ← slash

Count: 1   2   3   4

Each slash equals one beat. The chord name tells you which chord to play on each beat. Keep playing the same chord until a different chord name is shown.

The Staff and Treble Clef

Ukulele music is usually written on a five-line *staff* that has a *treble clef* at its beginning.

Treble clef

Bar Lines, Measures, and Time Signatures

Bar lines divide the staff into equal parts called *measures*. A *double bar line* is used at the end to show you the music is finished.

Measures are always filled with a certain number of beats. You know how many beats are in each measure by looking at the *time signature*, which is always at the beginning of the music. A $\frac{4}{4}$ time signature ("four-four time") means there are four equal beats in every measure. A $\frac{3}{4}$ time signature ("three-four time") means there are three equal beats.

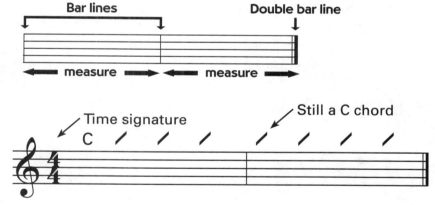

Bar lines   Double bar line

measure   measure

Time signature   Still a C chord

More Time to Strum

Play this example in $\frac{4}{4}$ time. It will sound the same as "Time to Strum!," which you played on page 6. Keep the beats even and count out loud.

Strum all four strings as you did before.

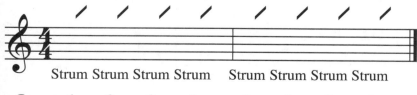

Strum Strum Strum Strum   Strum Strum Strum Strum

Count: 1   2   3   4   1   2   3   4

8

USING YOUR LEFT HAND

Hand Position

Learning to use your left-hand fingers starts with good hand position. Place your hand so your thumb rests comfortably in the middle of the back of the neck. Position your fingers on the front of the neck as if you are gently squeezing a ball between them and your thumb. Keep your elbow in and your fingers curved.

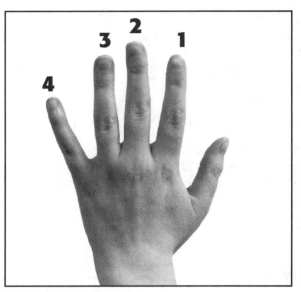

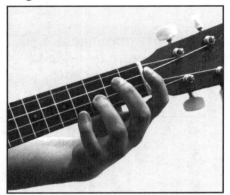

Keep elbow in and fingers curved.

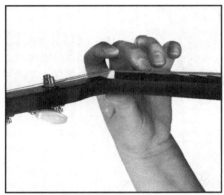

Like gently squeezing a ball between your fingers and thumb.

Finger numbers.

Placing a Finger on a String

When you press a string with a left-hand finger, make sure you press firmly with the tip of your finger and as close to the fret wire as you can without actually being right on it. Short fingernails are important! This will create a clean, bright tone.

RIGHT
Finger pressing the string down near the fret without actually being on it.

WRONG
Finger is too far from fret wire; tone is "buzzy" and indefinite.

WRONG
Finger is on top of fret wire; tone is muffled and unclear.

HOW TO READ CHORD DIAGRAMS

Chord diagrams show where to place your fingers. The example to the right shows finger 1 on the first string at the first fret. The "o"s above the second, third, and fourth strings tell you these strings are to be played open, meaning without pressing down on them with a left-hand finger.

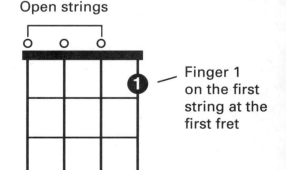

Open strings

Finger 1 on the first string at the first fret

THE C7 CHORD

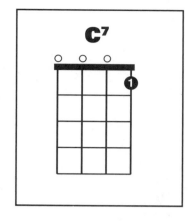

o = open string

Place your 1st finger in position, then play one string at a time.

- - - - - - - - - = string is not played

Play all four strings together:

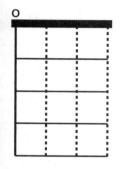 + 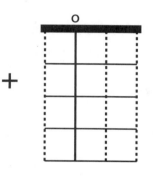 + 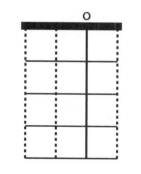 + 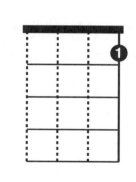 =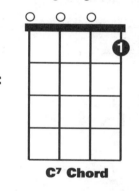

C⁷ Chord

Play slowly and evenly. Each slash mark ╱ means to repeat the previous chord. Strum downward for each chord name and slash mark. Use your finger or a pick.

1. 𝄞 4/4 C⁷ ╱ ╱ ╱ │ ╱ ╱ ╱ ╱ │ ╱ ╱ ╱ ╱ ‖*

Count : 1   2   3   4   1   2   3   4   1   2   3   4

2. 𝄞 3/4 C⁷ ╱ ╱ │ ╱ ╱ ╱ │ ╱ ╱ ╱ │ ╱ ╱ ╱ ‖

Count : 1   2   3   1   2   3   1   2   3   1   2   3

* Two thin lines show the end of a short example.

10

THE F CHORD

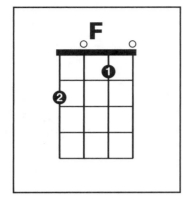

Place your 1st and 2nd fingers in position, then play one string at a time.

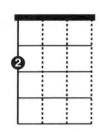 + 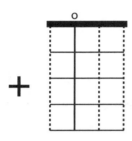 + 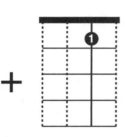 + 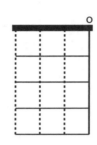 =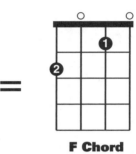

F Chord

1. 𝄞 4/4 F / / / | / / / / | / / / / ‖

2. 𝄞 3/4 F / / / | / / / | / / / | / / / ‖

INTRODUCING THE QUARTER REST

This sign indicates silence for one count. For a clearer effect, you may stop the sound of the strings by touching them lightly with the heel of the right hand.

Once you can play both the F and C7 chords clearly, try combining them.

1. 𝄞 4/4 F / / / | / / / / | C⁷ / / / | / / / / | F / / / | C⁷ / / / | F / / / | F ‖
HOLD

2. 𝄞 3/4 F / / / | / / / | C⁷ / / / | / / / | F / / / | C⁷ / / / | F / / / | / 𝄽 𝄽 ‖
COUNT: 1 REST REST

Ode to Joy

Theme from Beethoven's *Ninth Symphony*

This is one of the most popular melodies of all time. Play the chords and have your teacher or a friend play the melody. Sing along with the rest of the songs in the book.

* This is a *tempo sign*. A tempo sign tells you how fast or slow to play the music. *Moderato* is Italian and means to play at a moderate tempo.

12

Good Night Ladies

CHORDS USED IN THIS SONG

F   C⁷

Moderato

Good   night,   la - dies,   Good   night,   la - dies,

Good   night,   la - dies,   We're   going   to   leave   you   now.

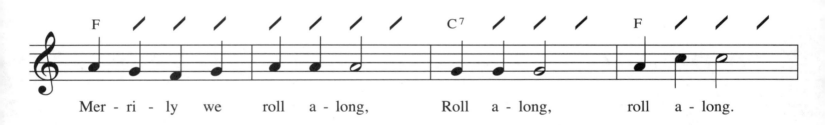

Mer - ri - ly   we   roll   a - long,   Roll   a - long,   roll   a - long.

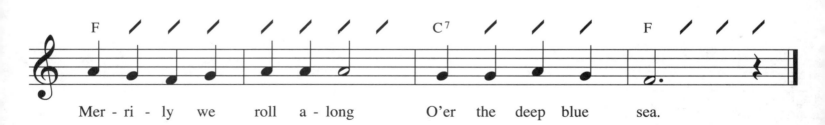

Mer - ri - ly   we   roll   a - long   O'er   the   deep   blue   sea.

Down in the Valley

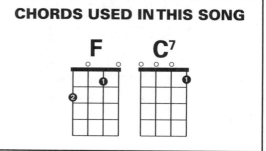

CHORDS USED IN THIS SONG

F   C⁷

Moderato

PLAY: F

Down in the val - ley, val - ley so

C⁷

low, Hang you head o -

C⁷   F

ver, hear the wind blow.

C⁷

Hear the wind blow, boys, hear the wind

C⁷

blow, Hang your head o -

C⁷   F

COUNT: 1 (2) (3)
(REST) (REST)

ver, hear the wind blow.

INCOMPLETE MEASURES

Not all pieces of music begin on the first beat. Sometimes, music begins with an incomplete measure called a *pickup*. If the pickup is one beat, often the last measure will only have three beats in $\frac{4}{4}$, or two beats in $\frac{3}{4}$.

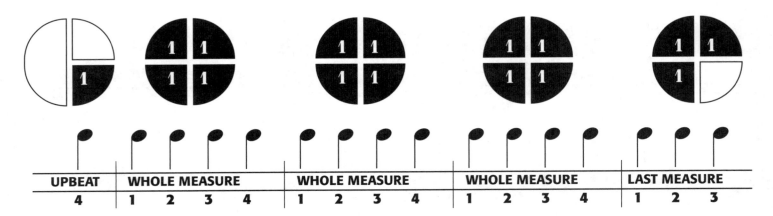

UPBEAT	WHOLE MEASURE	WHOLE MEASURE	WHOLE MEASURE	LAST MEASURE
4	1 2 3 4	1 2 3 4	1 2 3 4	1 2 3

CHORDS USED IN THIS SONG

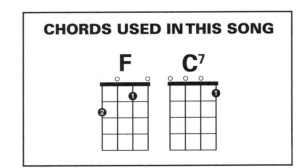

Clementine

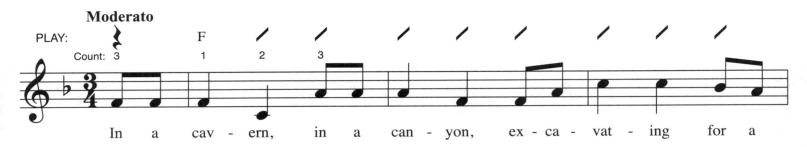

Moderato

PLAY:
Count: 3   1 2 3

In a cav - ern, in a can - yon, ex - ca - vat - ing for a

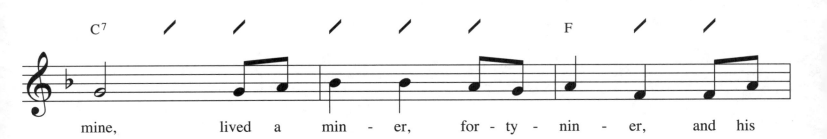

mine,   lived a min - er, for - ty - nin - er, and his

daugh - ter, Clem - en - tine. Oh my dar - lin', oh my

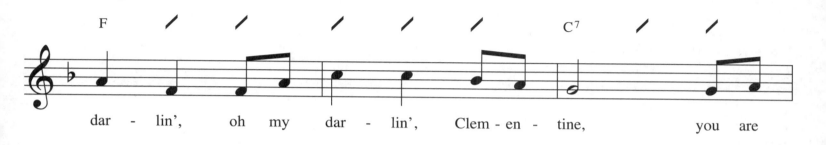

dar - lin', oh my dar - lin', Clem - en - tine, you are

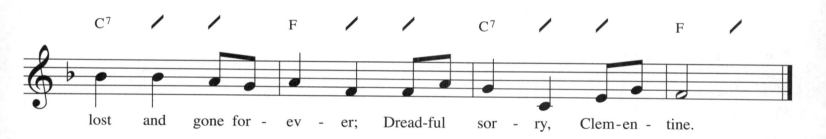

lost and gone for - ev - er; Dread-ful sor - ry, Clem-en - tine.

ADDITIONAL VERSES

Verse 2:
Light she was and like fairy,
And her shows were number nine,
Herring boxes without topses,
Sandals were for Clementine

Chorus:
Oh my darling, oh my darling,
Oh my darling, Clementine!
Thou art lost and gone forever
Dreadful sorry, Clementine.

Verse 3:
Drove she ducklings to the water
Every morning just at nine,
Hit her foot against a splinter,
Fell into the foaming brine.

Chorus:
Oh my darling, oh my darling
Oh my darling, Clementine!
Thou art lost and gone forever
Dreadful sorry, Clementine.

Verse 4:
Ruby lips above the water,
Blowing bubbles soft and fine,
But alas, I was no swimmer,
So I lost my Clementine.

Chorus:
Oh my darling, oh my darling
Oh my darling, Clementine
Thou art lost and gone forever,
Dreadful sorry, Clementine.

16

THE C CHORD

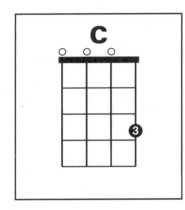 

Place your 3rd finger in position, then play one string at a time.

Play all four strings together:

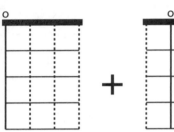 + 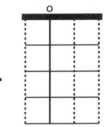 + 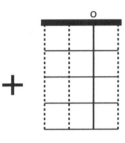 + 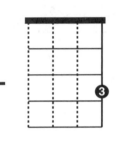 =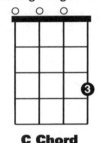

C Chord

Play slowly and evenly.

1. C

2. C

Now try these exercises. They combine all the chords you know.

1. C C⁷ F C F C

2. F C F C⁷ F

Tom Dooley

CHORDS USED IN THIS SONG

Moderato

Hang down your head, Tom Doo - ley. _____

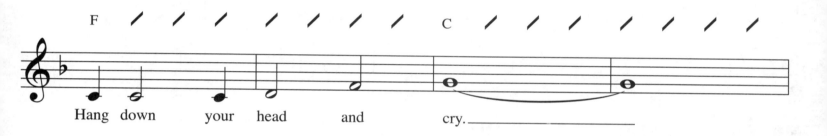

Hang down your head and cry. _____

Hang down your head, Tom Doo - ley. _____

Poor boy, you're bound to die. _____

THE G7 CHORD

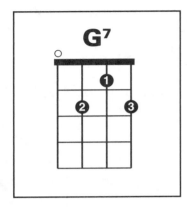

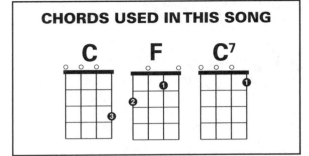

CHORDS USED IN THIS SONG

Place your 1st, 2nd, and 3rd fingers in position, then play one string at a time.

Play all four strings together:

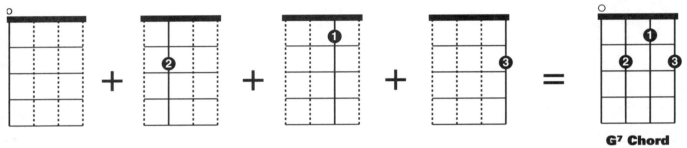

G7 Chord

USING G7 WITH OTHER CHORDS

Practice Tip

Before you play the next song, practice the following exercises. They will help you easily change chords. Play each exercise very slowly at first and gradually play them faster. Soon you will be able to move easily from chord to chord without missing a beat.

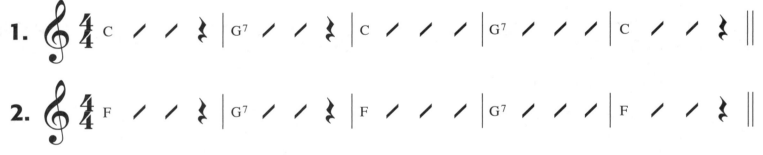

Aloha 'Oe

(Farewell to Thee)

To get used to playing the G7 chord, play this version of "Aloha 'Oe" (pronounced "oy") with just chords. Sing along with the melody.

This arrangement uses quarter note slashes that indicate to play one strum on each quarter note.

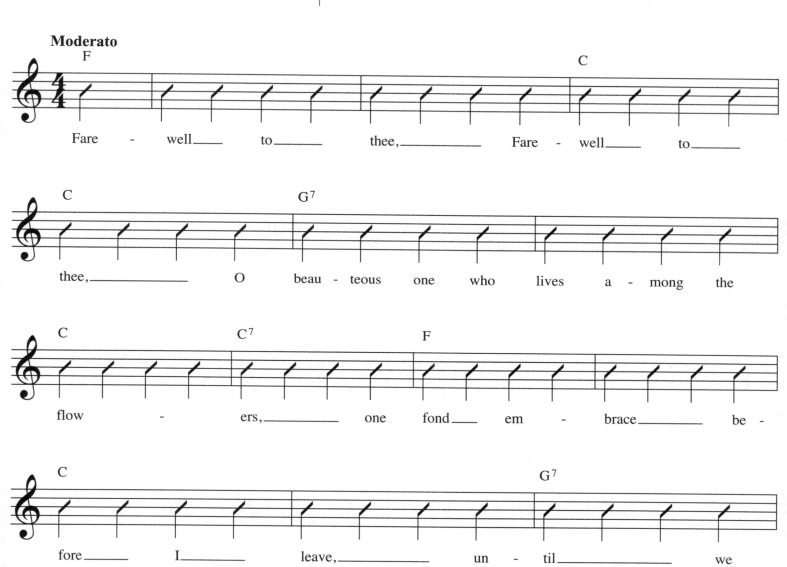

CHORDS USED ON THIS PAGE

C   G7   C7   F

When the Saints Go Marching In

Allegro *

PLAY: C

Oh, when the saints go march-ing in.

Oh, when the saints go march-ing in.

Lord, how I want to be in that num-ber

When the saints go march-ing in.

The Streets of Laredo

Moderato

PLAY:

As I walked out in the streets of La - re - do, as

I walked out in La - re - do one day, I

spied a young cow - boy all dressed in white lin - en, all

dressed in white lin - en as cold as the clay.

Allegro means to play fast.

THE G CHORD

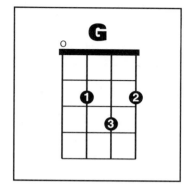 

Place your 1st, 2nd, and 3rd fingers in position, then play one string at a time.

Play all four strings together:

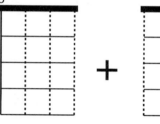 + 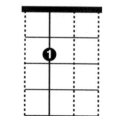 + 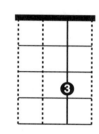 + 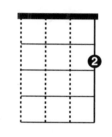 +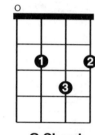

G Chord

THE D7 CHORD

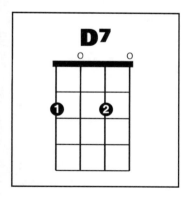 

Place your 1st and 2nd fingers in position, then play one string at a time.

Play all four strings together:

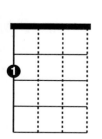 + 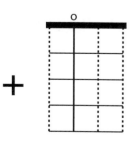 + 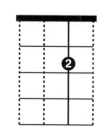 + 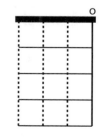 +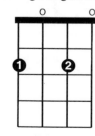

D7 Chord

Jingle Bells

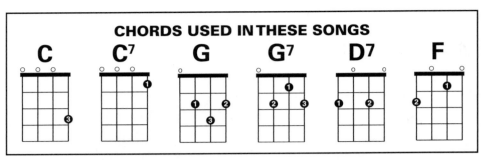

CHORDS USED IN THESE SONGS

Allegro

Jin - gle bells! Jin - gle bells! Jin - gle all the way!

Oh, what fun it is to ride in a one - horse o - pen sleigh! _____

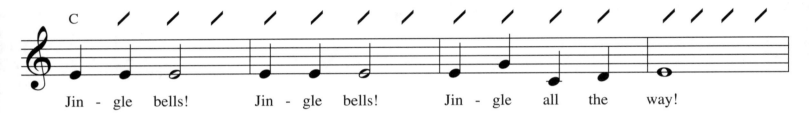

Jin - gle bells! Jin - gle bells! Jin - gle all the way!

Oh, what fun it is to ride in a one - horse o - pen sleigh! _____

Over the Rainbow

The greatest ukulele version of this song was recorded in 1993 by legendary Hawaiian uke player and singer Iz.

Words by E. Y. Harburg
Music by Harold Arlen

Moderato

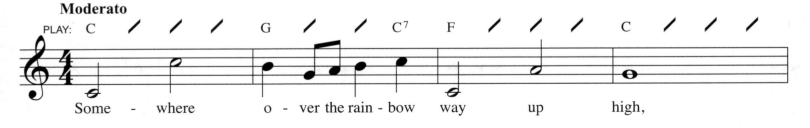

Some - where o - ver the rain - bow way up high,

UKULELE CHORD DICTIONARY

Congratulations, you've just finished *It's Ukulele Time*. You are now ready to learn to read music and play many more songs in *Alfred's Basic Ukulele Method 1*. Below are some chords to learn that will get you started playing sheet music.

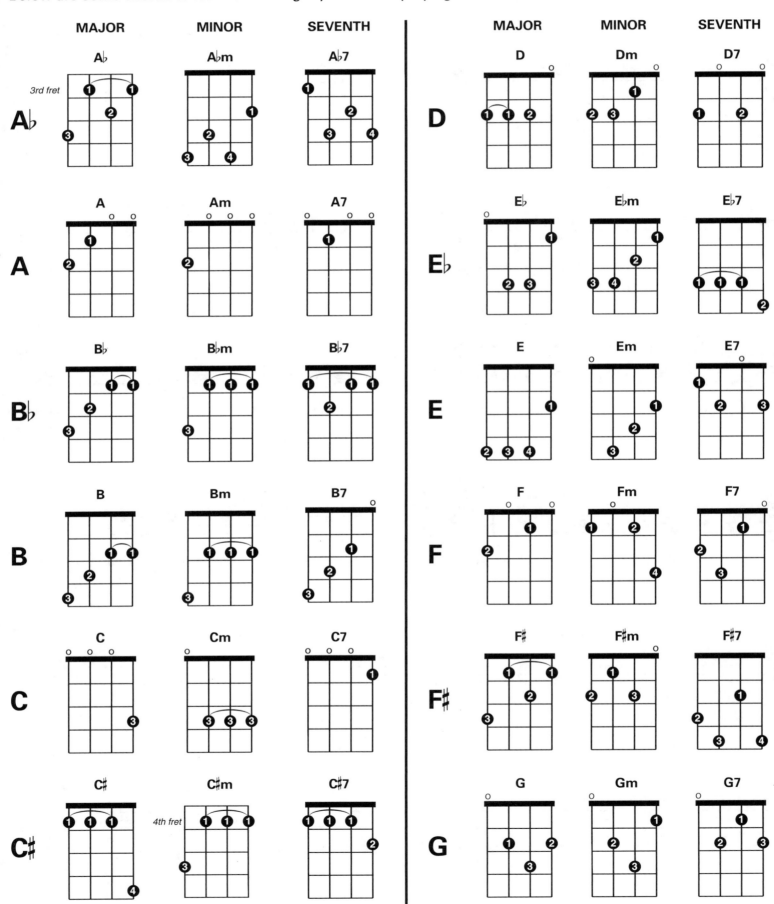